STEPPING STONES

By Lucy Knisley

For
Taylor
&
Chelsea

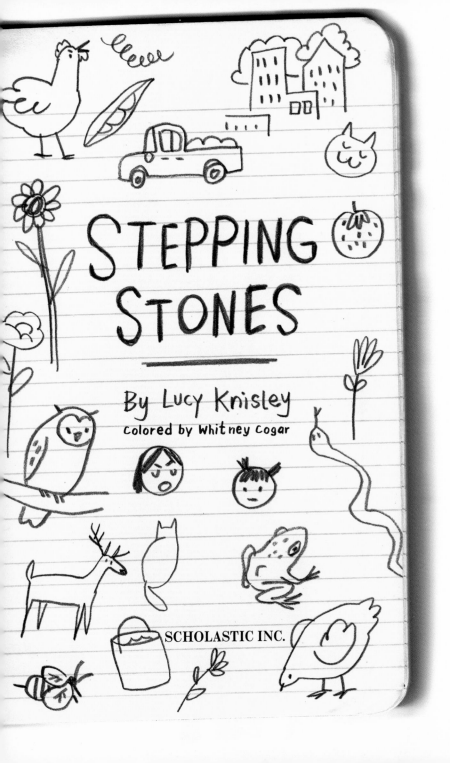

STEPPING STONES

By Lucy Knisley

Colored by Whitney Cogar

SCHOLASTIC INC.

No part of this publication may be reproduced, stored in a retrieval system, or transmitted in any form or by any means, electronic, mechanical, photocopying, recording, or otherwise, without written permission of the publisher. For information regarding permission, write to Random House Children's Books, Permissions Department, 1745 Broadway, 15th Floors, New York, NY 10019.

ISBN 978-1-338-70379-5

12 11 10 9 8 7 6 5 4 3 2 1   20 21 22 23 24 25

Printed in the U.S.A.   40

First Scholastic printing, September 2020

Designed by Patrick Crotty
Colored by Whitney Cogar

Stepping Stones was drawn with Blackwing *602* pencils on bristol and colored digitally.

Chapter
One

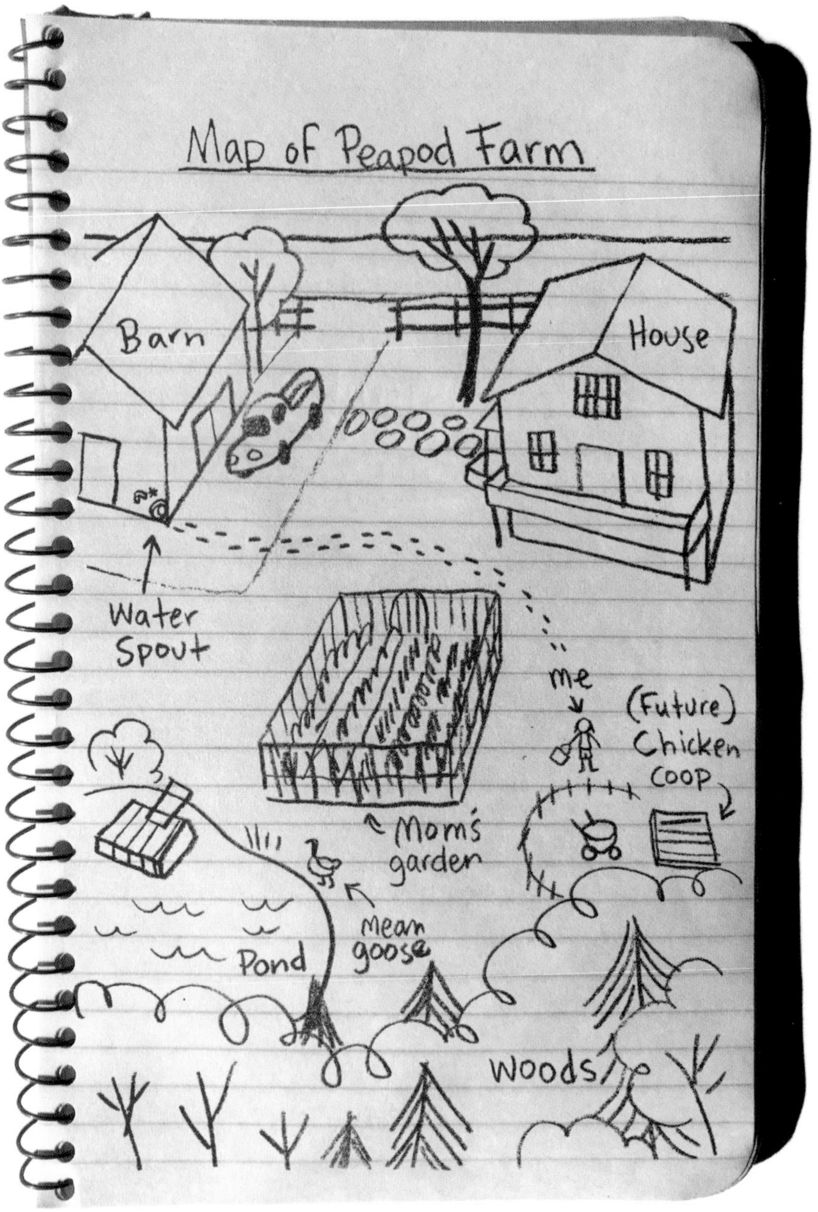

Map of Peapod Farm

Barn

House

Water Spout

me

(Future) Chicken Coop

Mom's garden

Pond

Mean goose

Woods

POP

GASP

Mew!

Barn kittens!

ZOOM

ZOOM

16

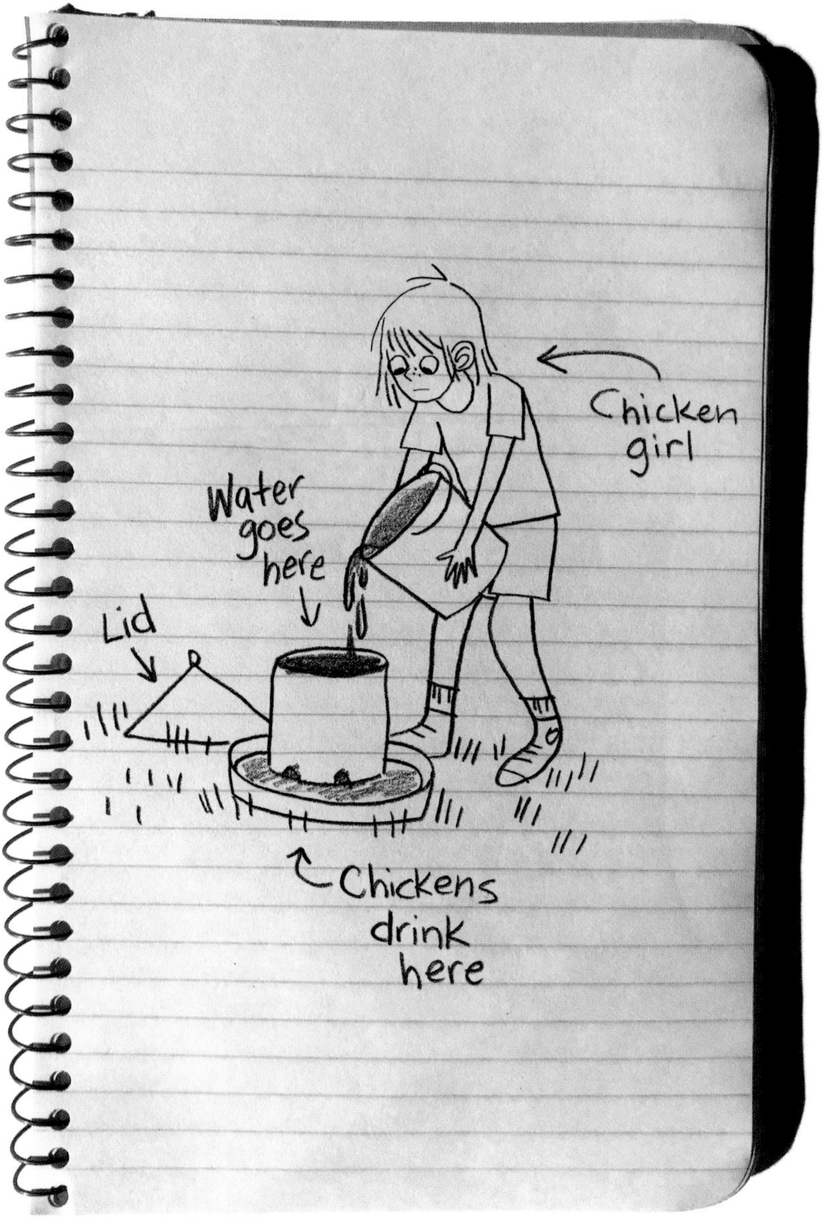
Chicken girl
Water goes here
Lid
Chickens drink here

Chapter
Two

22

23

URGH!

Mom?

Aaaargh!

Hey, Mom, what's going on?

Those darn deer got into the garden again and ate all my lettuces!

What?

How?

Six-foot-tall fence

They're monsters! Last week it was my carrots! Why didn't anyone warn me about the deer up here?

Just watch out! Those deer will eat everything!

Ha, okay!

uhh...

uhh, okay. I'm gonna—

Did you lay the straw in the chicken yard yet?

um.

Jen, the chickens will be here any day! The coop needs to be ready. I've got my hands full here.

Jeez, okay, fine!

Thank you!

These had better be good eggs.

RING

Hello, um, Peapod Farm.

Hello, yes, this is the post office calling. Your delivery is ready for pickup.

We need to come to the post office?

Doesn't the mail usually get delivered?

Yep, this is a special kind of package.

Here, listen.

PEEP PEEP PEEP PEEP

PEEP PEEP PEEP PEEP PEEP PEEP

POOP

WIPE

Okay, kiddo, you hop in the back and make sure they're okay.

I get to ride in the back of the truck?

Yep, just be careful back there.

Phew!

CRASH SPLASH
PEEP
PEEP PEEP

JENNY! Come help your mom get the berries in the truck!

I'm coming!

Are you excited about market? Your first real job!

What about when I worked for Dad at his office?

That doesn't count— you were inside all day!

Wait, do we need two blackboards for the stand?

PEAPOD FARM
BERRIES
GRANOLA
RHUBAR

PEAPOD FARM
BERRIES-$7
GRANOLA-$8
RHUBARB-$5
FLOWERS-$6
ASPARAGUS-$5

Okay, Jen, I'm gonna run over to talk to the owner of Hillcroft Farms next door.

You're in charge till I get back, okay?

Wait, alone?

Hello! I'll take three pints of goldenberries. Do you have change for a fifty?

uh...

uh, yes, um, here you go, uh...

39

Excuse me, Tom.

uh, we have a customer, and I, uh...

Sorry about that.

No problem!

I thought we talked about this.

Your dad said he's been doing your flash cards with you.

I know—I know my sixes pretty well, but...

You've got to be able to make change if you're going to work at the market.

Remember what I told you about counting down from the total?

I know, I know...

I can't be here all the time, Jen, and Walter has to work at the farm.

I know.

keep at it, okay? I know you'll get it.

RING
RING
RING
RING

Hi, you've reached Sam MacInnes. I'm in Toronto on business, so please contact my office if you need to speak with me. Thanks. BEEP!

oh yeah.

CLICK

Chapter
Three

next weekend

SLAM

Well, girls, here it is!

Peapod Farm!

What do you think?

Welcome, Andy and Reese!

59

Good luck, girls!

Okay, Jen, why don't you give Andy the rundown.

I've got to go speak to the market manager about our fee. I'll be back in a bit.

Peapod Farm
Berries $7
Flowers $4

Okay, um, the flowers are four dollars a bunch. The berries are seven a box.

We have to put the berries in the bag carefully, or we'll squish them.

Why don't you just give them the box, to keep the berries safe?

We could, but then we'd run out of boxes.

Mom says not to, unless they ask.

Hm.

Fine, but that's not how I'd do it.

Mom's granola is eight dollars.

Eight? That's a lot for a bag of cereal.

She makes it herself.

We should do a special sale! Buy a box of berries and get granola twenty-five percent off.

Uh...

I'm gonna write it on the board.

Hello there! Is that a special on the granola? I can't quite read it.

Yes! Buy a box of berries and get twenty-five percent off the granola.

That's a great deal! I'll take it.

Excellent!

You can pay my associate here.

Here you go.

Thank you for your business!

68

That's three PM! Time to pack up.

Hello there. What do you think of my bees?

They're so cool!

You work at a stand, too, right?

Yep. Over there.

You guys had a special today, didn't you?

Yeah.

Well I've got a special, too. A free honey stick to a fellow farmer!

Thanks!

Okay, we're all packed up. Hop in, everybody.

Chapter
Four

next weekend

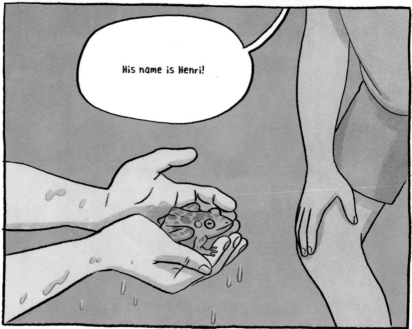

MOM!

She's in the shower.

What's up?

Andy let my frog get away!

It wasn't YOUR frog!

IT WAS, TOO! I CAUGHT IT!

I did, too!

And I NAMED him!

SHE WAS A GIRL!

okay, calm down.

Jenny, you've gotten used to being the only kid around here. You've got to learn to share and take turns.

But...

But...

I know, it's a lot to get used to with the move and the girls spending the weekends here.

Yeah.

There are gonna be a lot of bumps along the way, but we'll all get through it. You just have to be a good hostess.

What?

These girls are away from their mom. This farm is new to them, too. We need to be gracious and try to share our things with them.

But she's such a mean, bossy know-it-all!

Chapter

Five

Next weekend

Hi, girls! How was market this week?

Great!

I introduced some new sales techniques into our business, and people seemed to like it a lot!

Jen dropped a whole bag of granola and spilled it.

I couldn't help it! I was trying to help like five customers!

Maybe if you got a little more organized, you could handle it.

You already can't even handle working the cash box.

What? Jenny, is that true?

She has trouble with the math.

You know, sweetie, you really should work on that. You ought to be able to make change if you're going to work the market.

Get back here, young lady.

Come on, Jen.

I'll walk home!

Sweetie, be reasonable.

Have it your way, kid.

RUSTLE
RUSTLE

RUSTLE
RUSTLE

SIGH

WAHHH!!!

What's going on?

WHAAHH!!

Hey, Reese, you okay?

I get it.

I'm not crazy about this place, either.

Really?

But you're like... a farmer.

You wanna hear a funny story about when I first moved here?

Sure.

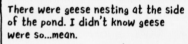
I went down to the pond to see if there were any turtles there.

There were geese nesting at the side of the pond. I didn't know geese were so...mean.

They made this horrible hissing sound, trying to scare me away from their nest.

I tried to climb a tree to get away from them...

...but I didn't know the tree had a hornet's nest in it.

I got stung on the eye! I fell out of the tree into a big mud puddle!

Yeah! You could draw a special logo for the farm!

Like a goat! Or a peapod, I guess.

uh.
Yeah! I could do that.

Thanks, kiddo.

You're a big help.

RUFFLE

I'm not much help at market.

That's not true.

Chapter
Six

Next weekend

Ya don't just wanna yank on it.

You gotta be gentle.

You take your thumb and forefinger and wrap 'em around the top of the teat.

Then you close your fist toward your palm, like so.

So! Who wants to go first?

Okay, then, step right up.

Cool!

I wanna try!

Thanks for showing the girls the ropes, Steve.

No problem, Walt. It's what neighbors do.

You wanna give it a try, Reese?

Thanks again, Steve. Mike.

Anytime, neighbor. Our nephew's about their age. He's coming to stay with us in a couple of weeks. You should bring the girls by to meet him.

Okay, girls, let's get home. We've got a big project ahead of us.

Do you think that cow would eat her own butter?

Ew!

Oh, and one more thing.

Watch out for rattlesnakes.

Mr. Fisher was telling me there are a few of them back there in the woods, so be careful.

Okay, have fun!

Why do you think your dad said that?

About the snakes?

Yeah.

Who knows. He's funny like that.

I don't think it's funny.

You just don't understand his humor.

I guess not.

He used to be a lawyer. He's very smart.

Okay.

But I guess... he shouldn't joke about snakes. Maybe he doesn't know how scared you are.

Do you think your dad and my mom will get married?

I don't know.

It would be weird, I guess.

Yeah. Pretty weird.

But also it would be cool to have sisters.

It's been kinda... nice to have some kids around when you and Reese come for weekends.

Sisters are overrated.

You have to share everything with them, and you fight a lot.

But I like coming to visit, too.

I guess we'd be stepsisters, but the only stepsisters I know are the ones from *Cinderella*.

Haha! Yeah! The evil ones!

Shovel those wood chips, Cinderandy! Clean the chicken coop, Cinderjen!

Ha!

Whoa!

Look out!

Huh?

ZOOM

Oh no.

Reese!

Chapter
Seven

next weekend

SNIP

Are the chickens supposed to be in here?

Yes! They're helping by eating the bad bugs that try to eat the flowers and veggies.

151

I get to come to market this week, too!

Uh-huh.

I'm gonna be the flower girl!

That's for a wedding, not market, silly.

156

Well done, Reese!

Excuse me.

Peapod Farm

I...

The signs are my job.

Oh, come on.

You're not the only one who can write on a chalkboard.

Honestly, Jenny, if you worked a little harder in math, you could work the till with Andy.

Then you could *really* be a help to your mom here at market.

Hey, where are you girls going?

Hey! We still need to pack up!

Chapter
Eight

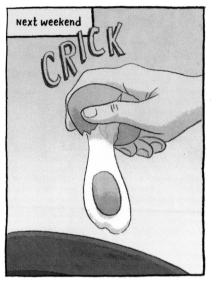

There were five this morning! One for each of us.

One for Reese, for always being a chicken cheerleader...

One for Walter, for building the coop.

About time they showed some gratitude for that!

One for Andy, for fixing their water so they didn't keep knocking it over.

I re-engineered the trough system!

One for Jen, for cleaning up after them every day.

This egg had better be good!

And one for me, for being the cook!

Welp, that was a pretty good egg.

The best egg!

Okay, let's head to market! Dishes in the sink!

I spent the morning putting twine up to keep your garden from getting chomped.

Thank you!

It broke my heart to see you fighting a losing battle against the local fauna.

Maybe now I can try lettuce again!

Mmm, lettuce! Do they make pizza plants?

Daddy! That's silly!

Hello there!

Oh, hello, Mr. Fisher. Can I interest you in our special today?

Pea Pod @ Farm♥
BERRIES-$7
GRANOLA-$8
FLOWERS-$6

Haha, thanks, but your parents give me plenty already!

You lot are good neighbors to have around!

I just wanted to introduce you to our nephew, Eddie.

He comes to help us with the harvest.

TUG

FISH
FA

184

Thought you girls might like to know another farm kid in our little neck of the woods.

Hi.

FISHER FARMS

Hello!

Hi.

Hi!

Would you care to try a sample of our delicious granola?

Uh

okay.

So are you all, um...sisters?

Um

Well...

Err

Stepsisters, basically.

But we're not evil!

Sort of, part-time sisters.

Okay.

Walt says you girls spotted a rattler in the woods behind the farm a couple of weeks ago!

It was as long as me! And it had huge fangs!

We barely made it out alive!

We're not going back there anytime soon, that's for sure.

No way!

Well, glad you're all okay! Nice to see you girls!

Nice to meet you! See you around.

189

we have to winterize the chicken coop, and plow the summer crops to make way for winter ones, and we told the neighbors we'd help with their pumpkin patch.

SIGH

But we don't have to do any of that today, do we?

THUD
THUD

...gs that are O.K.
...about the country:

) Swimming!

②. The food

③. Riding in the truck

④. Mom is happy

⑤. My part-time sisters

A Note From The Author

When I was a kid, my parents split up and my mom and I moved from New York City to a little farm in the country.

She wanted to grow flowers and berries and get her hands dirty. I wanted to read comic books INSIDE where it was CLEAN, but sometimes when you're a kid, you're just along for the ride.

Mom

Me

I wasn't always thrilled with my mom's decision to become a super farmer lady, but I didn't have much of a choice about becoming a not-so-super farm kid.

Then my mom got a boyfriend. He was loud, bossy, and annoying. I'd never met such an annoying grown-up! And his daughters! A loud, bossy kid and her whiny little sister! Suddenly, I was sharing my room every weekend with these total strangers.

One of the worst things about being a kid is finding yourself in these situations where you have no control over the decisions the adults are making that affect you. But sometimes it's also one of the best things— to find yourself in a situation you couldn't possibly have chosen for yourself, totally at sea. It can sometimes bring unexpected beauty, and introduce strangers that become family.

My "Andy" is still loud and bossy, but she's also brilliant and funny. My "Reese" is much less whiney now, and much cooler than all of us, as she has always been.

My "Walter" was both annoying and beloved until his dying day.

My mom is still getting her hands dirty and loving her life in the country, and I am so thankful to her for forcing me to endure such a beautiful childhood full of rattlesnakes and ponds and lots more stories to tell.

(Another little note)

Big shocker: I am bad at math.

$$\begin{array}{r} 4 \\ \times 7 \\ \hline 28 \end{array}$$

I'm not just BAD at math, though; I'm dyscalculiac! It's a little like dyslexia, but rather than reading, this one impairs your ability to process numbers and magnitude.

When I graduated, I breathed a sigh of relief that I'd never have to do math again, but then I became a comic artist and had to learn how to measure and divide a page of panels! It was like algebra RETURNING FROM THE GRAVE TO HAUNT ME.

1²3⁴⁵ °o° I'M BACK!

Being "good" at something is less important than trying or practicing. After all, I became a comic artist after years and YEARS of practicing my drawing and writing. And I'm much better at math than I used to be! My "Andy," of course, is an engineer, and sometimes she has to draw diagrams and she's rotten at it, but she's getting better, too. Who'da thunk it?

Acknowledgments:

Thank you to Taylor, Chelsea, and Georgia.
Thank you to the Rhinebeck Farmers' Market.
Thank you to my fellow children of divorce.

Thank you to my publishing team at Random
House Graphic! Gina Gagliano and
Whitney Leopard and Patrick Crotty!
Thank you to Whitney Coger
for beautiful colors.
Thank you to Holly Bemiss
for being my champion.

Thank you to bees for your honey and
gardens for your flowers and bushes for
your berries and cows for your milk and
barns for your kittens.

Thank you to Warren, who I miss and who
would have been very sweet and very
annoying about this whole book.

Thank you to John and Pal,
who are my faves.

Author shown with pencil stubs
used during the making of this book!

About The Author

Lucy Knisley grew up with one foot in New York City and the other on an upstate farm.

An only child with divorced parents, she was an avid comic book and fantasy reader, who began to navigate the unfamiliar world of step-familial melodrama when she was eleven.

She graduated from the School of the Art Institute of Chicago, followed by the Center for Cartoon Studies, and began publishing graphic novels (a travelogue) at the age of twenty-two.

She has always tried to use her work to make people feel less alone through her honest and confessional comics. Her topics range from travel, adulthood, ailing grandparents, foreign romance, wedding planning, food, and reproductive health.

She lives in Chicago, where she likes riding her bike with her son and partner, and reading fantasy novels and comic books.